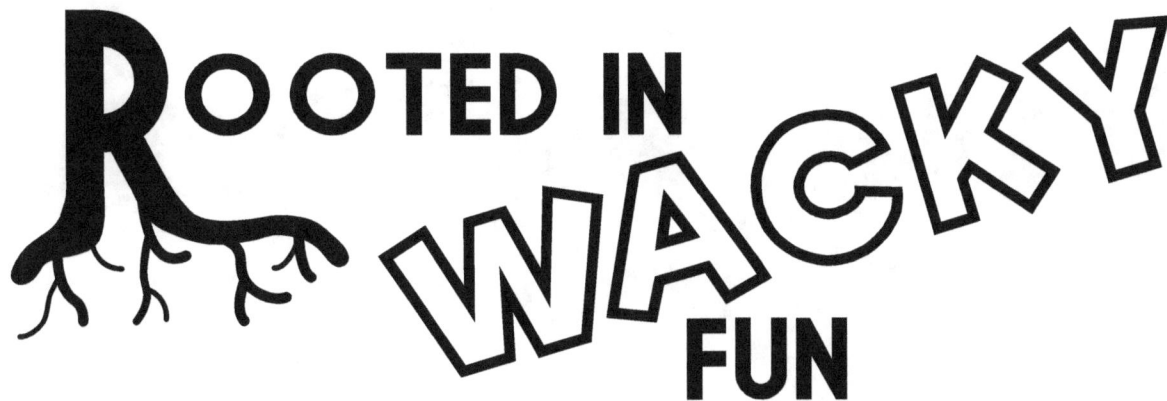

A coloring adventure for all

Jeanette Wummel

Coloring Tip:

When coloring with markers place a piece of paper between pages to prevent bleeding to your next design.

Acknowledgments

I can never say thank you to all the people who have supported and encourage me in making my dreams come true.

Follow me

Website/Blog:
www.TheRootsofDesign.com

Facebook:
www.facebook.com/TheRootsofDesign

Instagram:
www.instagram.com/therootsofdesign

Twitter:
https://twitter.com/Roots_Of_Design

Etsy:
www.RootsDesign.Etsy.com

Patreon:
www.patreon.com/RootsOfDesign

Copyright

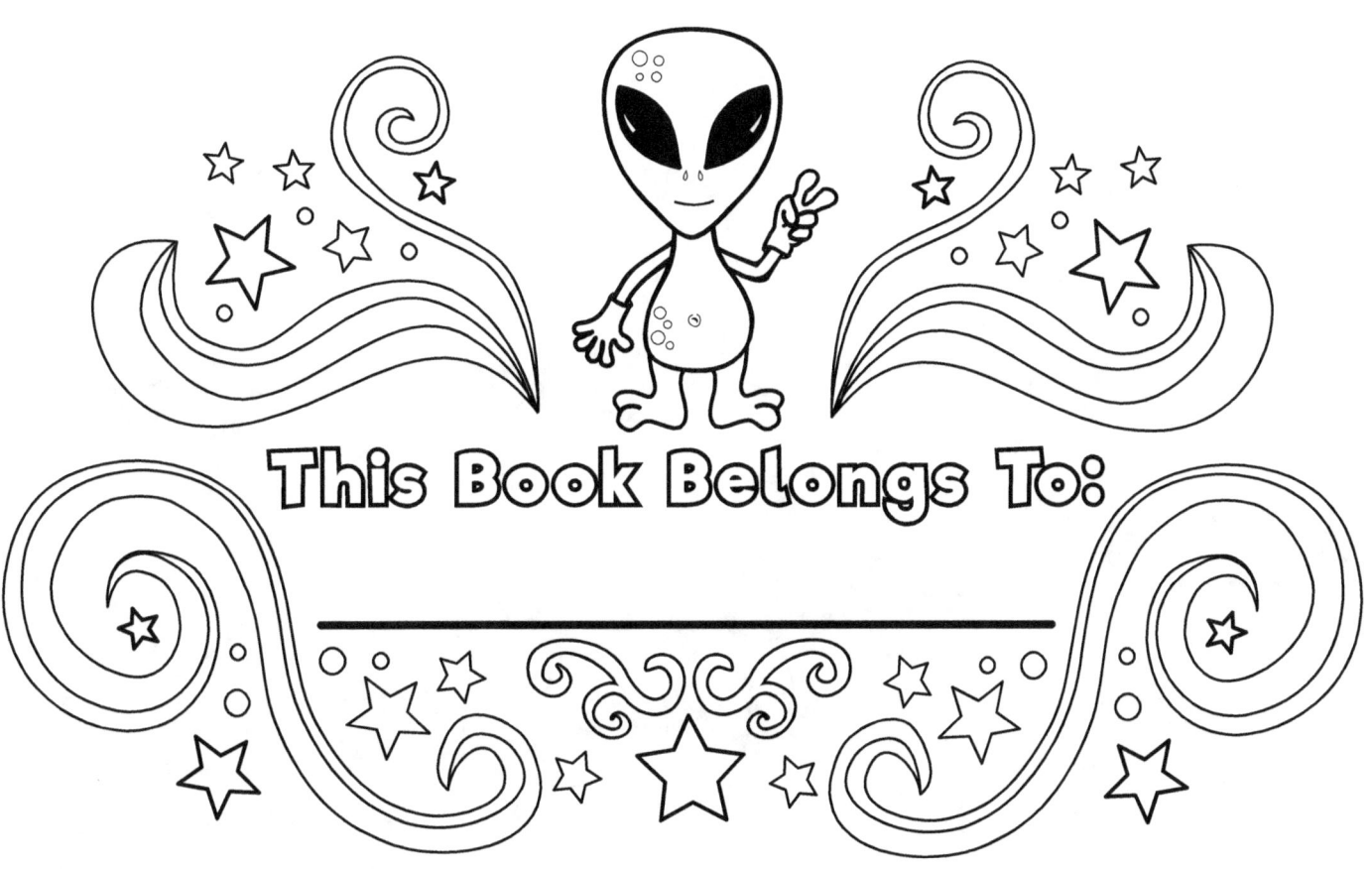

This Book Belongs To:

_____

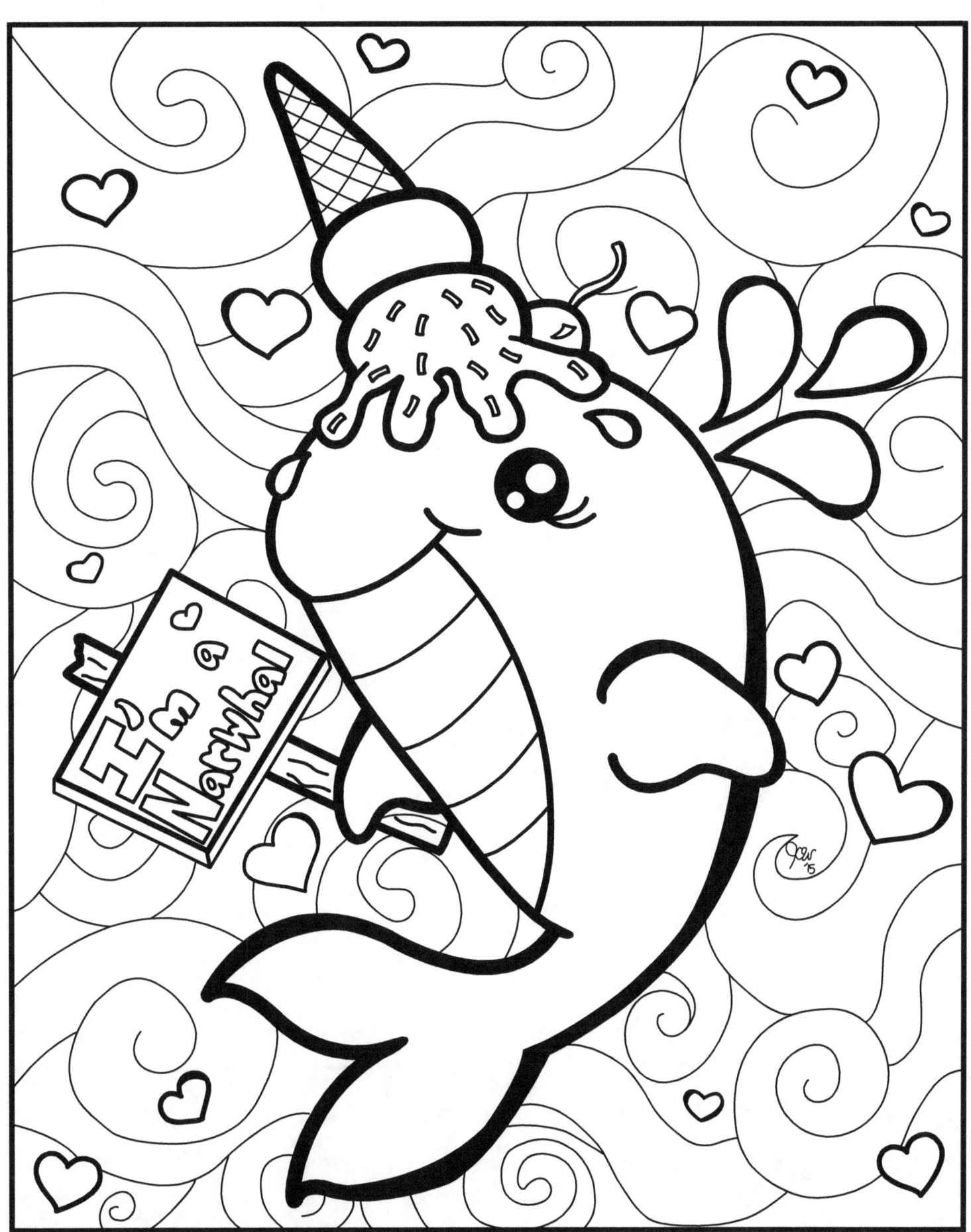

I'm a Narwhal

Ice Cream Whale

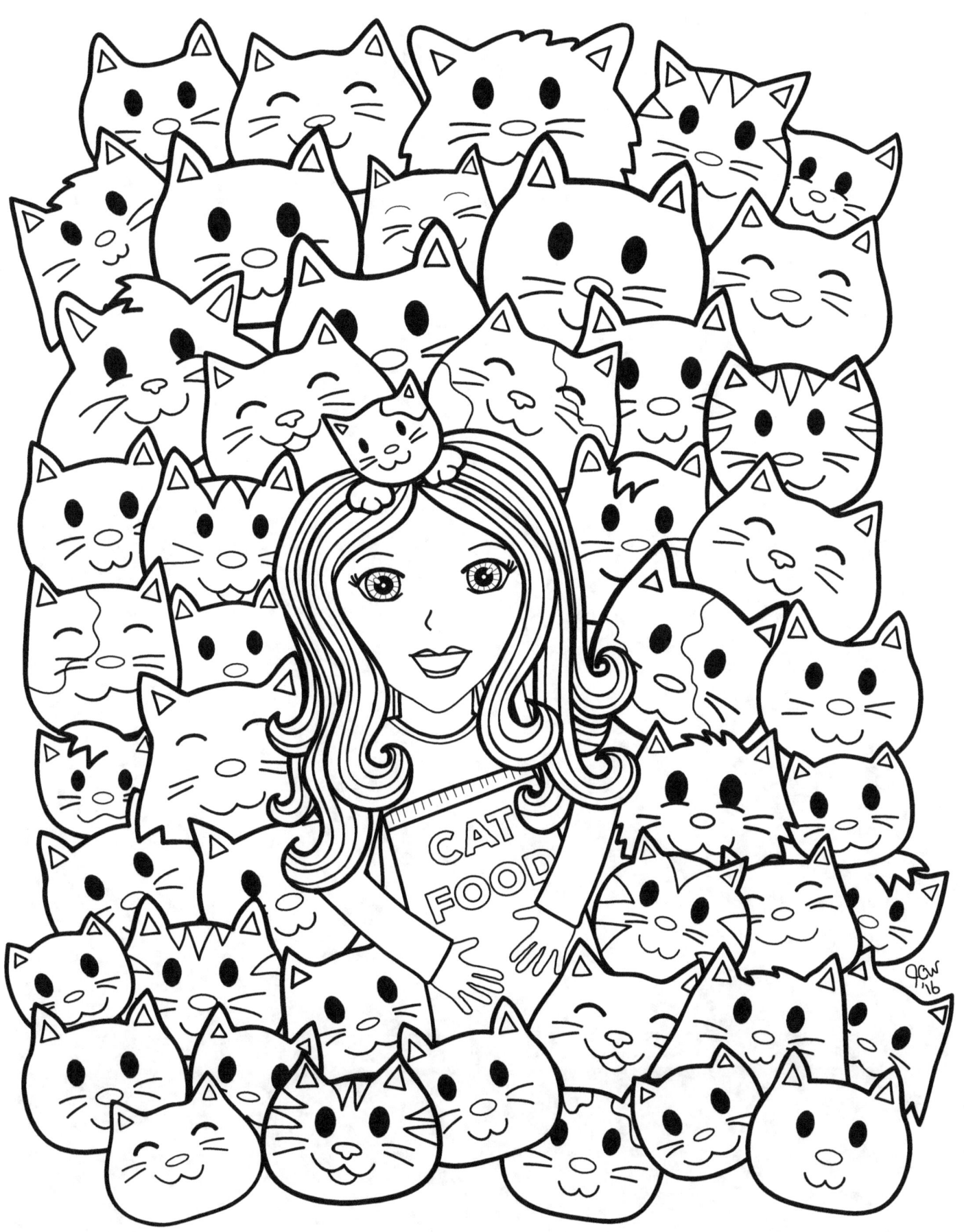

Crazy Cat Lady

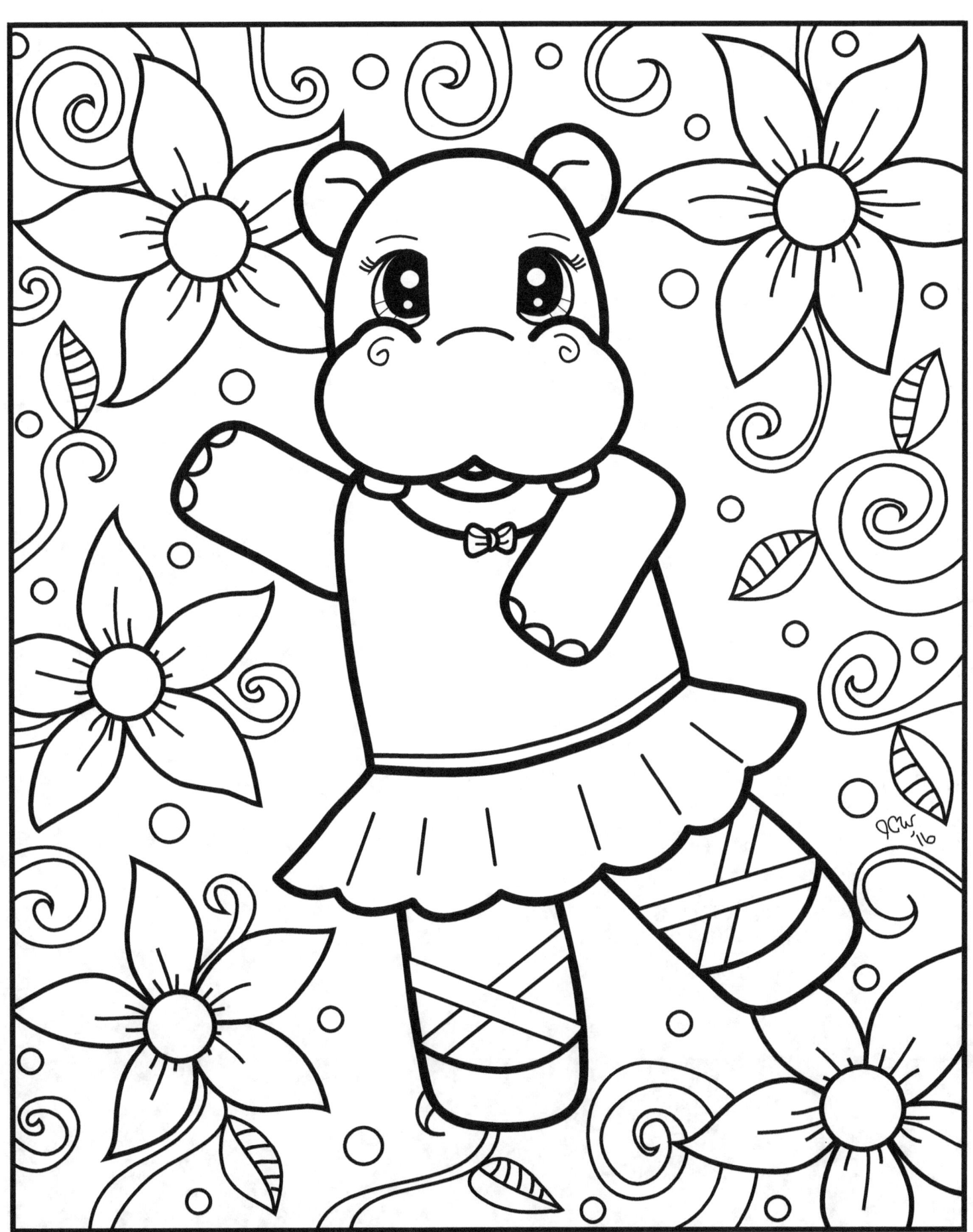

Dancing Hippo

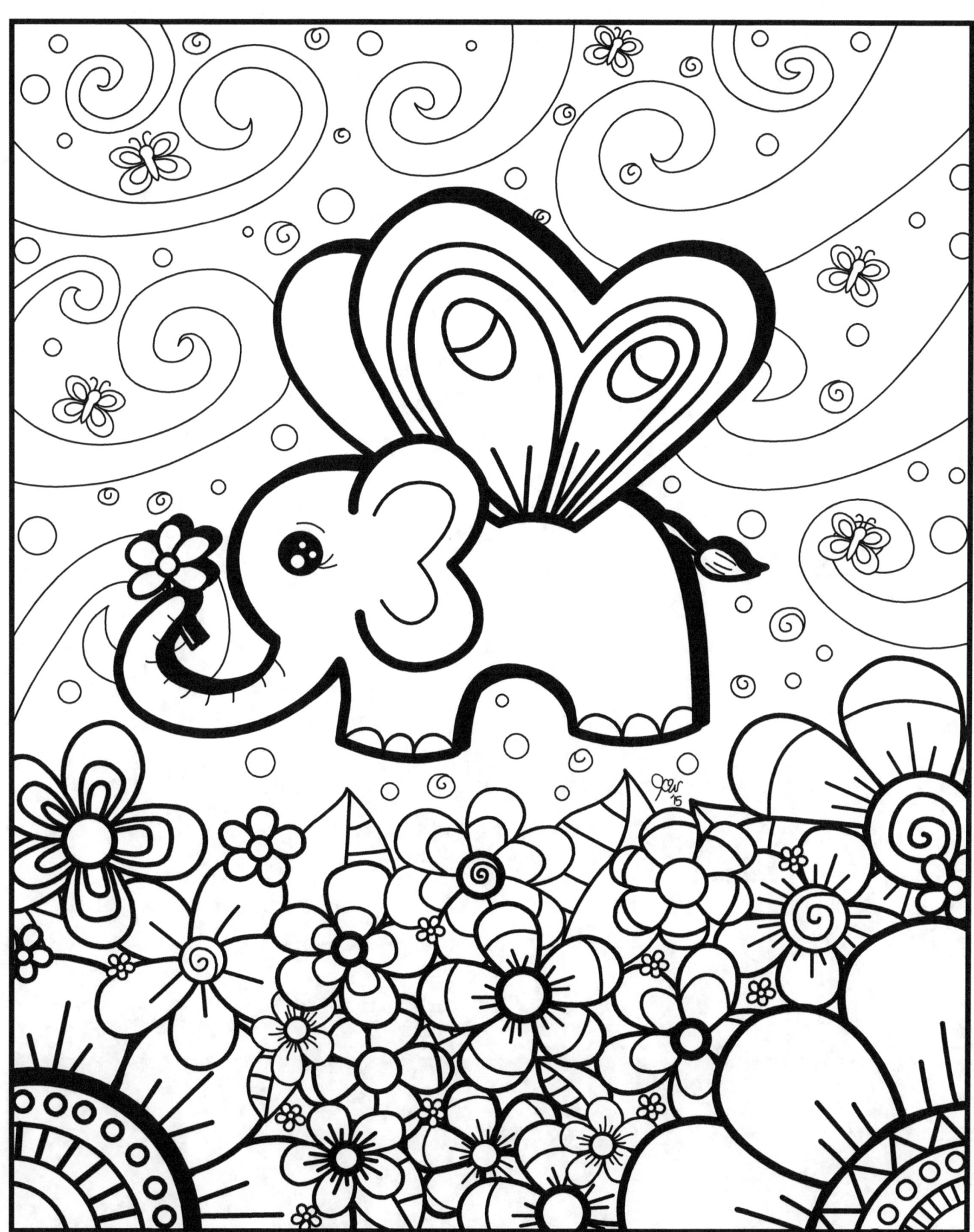

Ele-fly

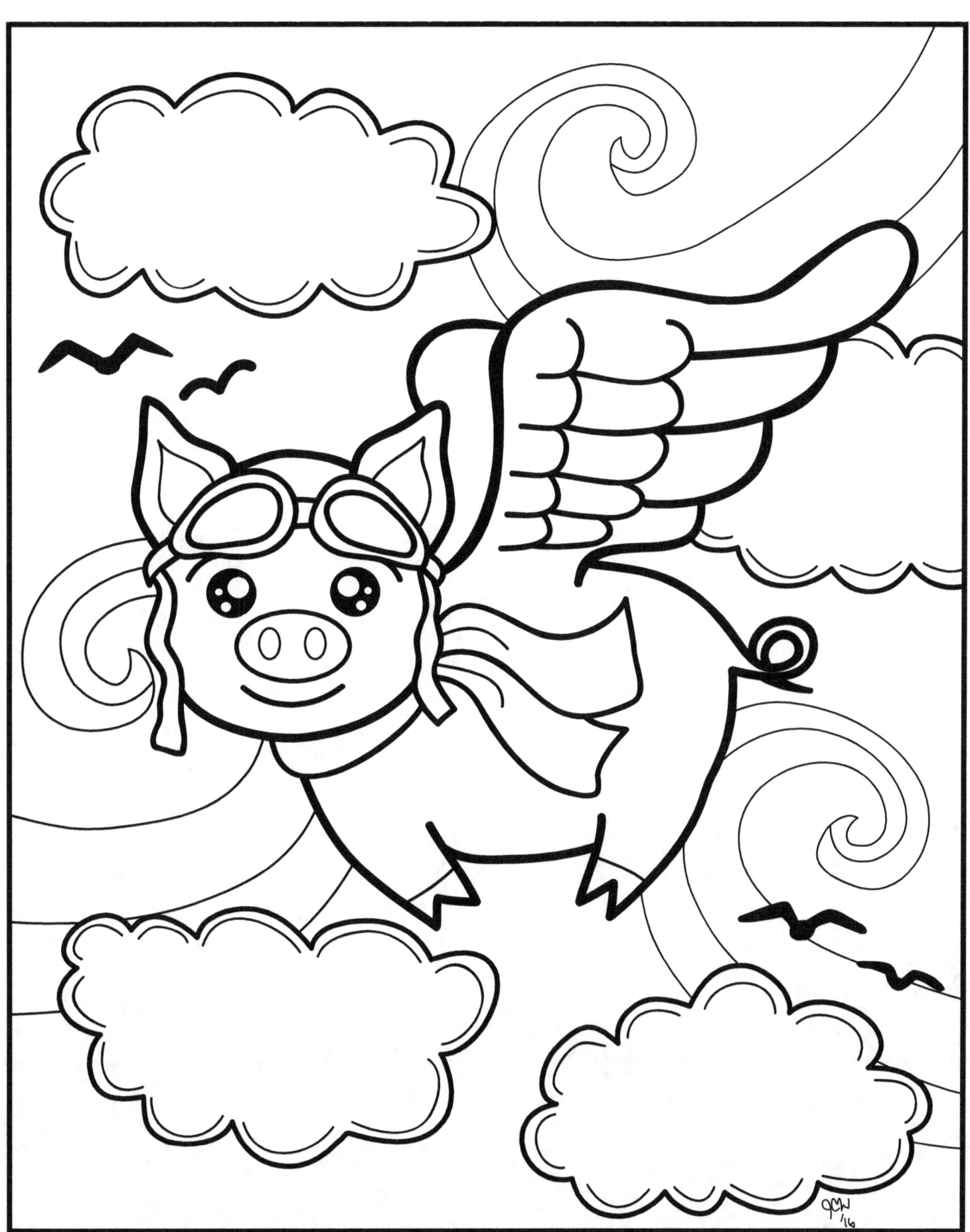

When Pigs Fly

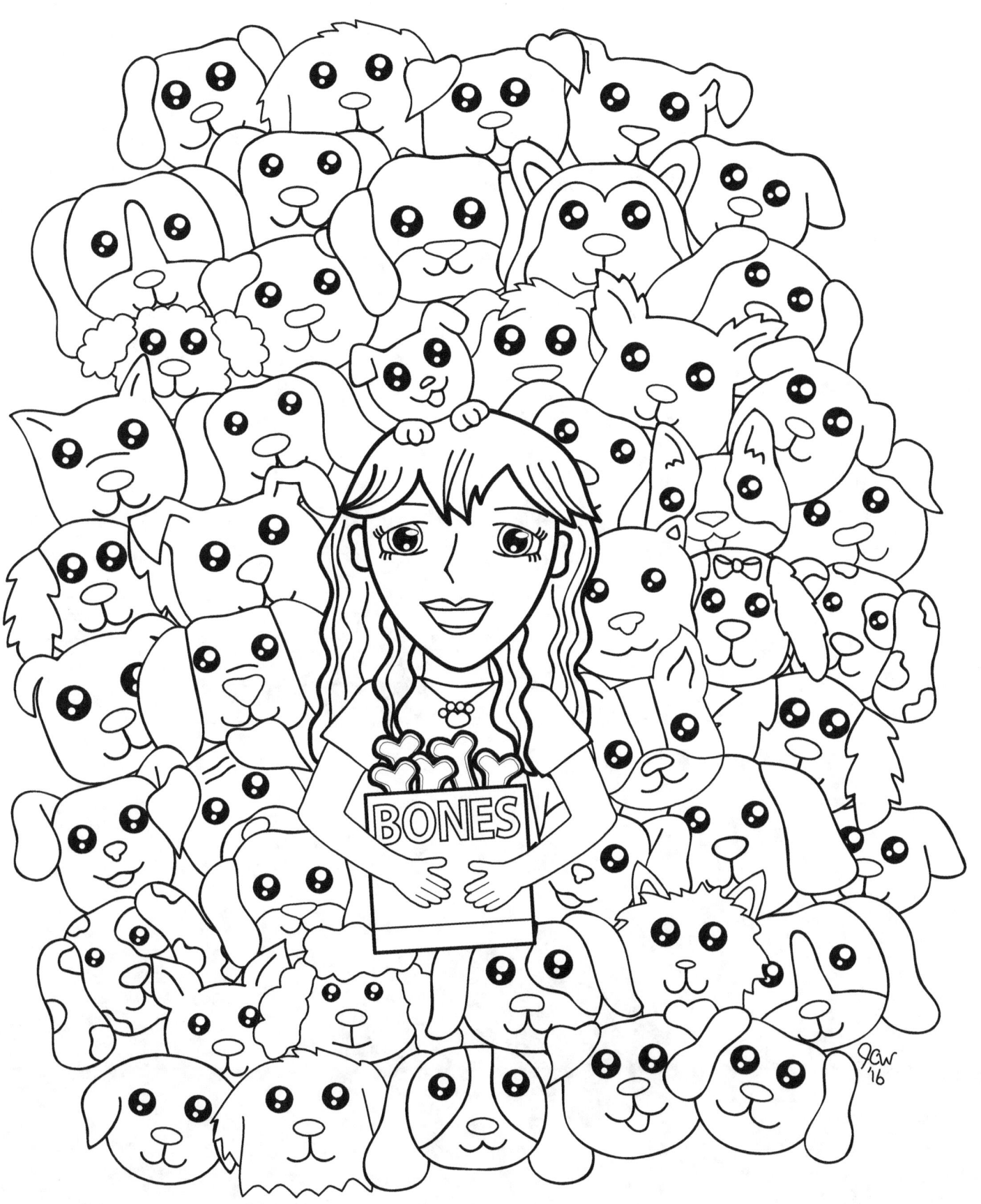

Dog Gone Crazy!

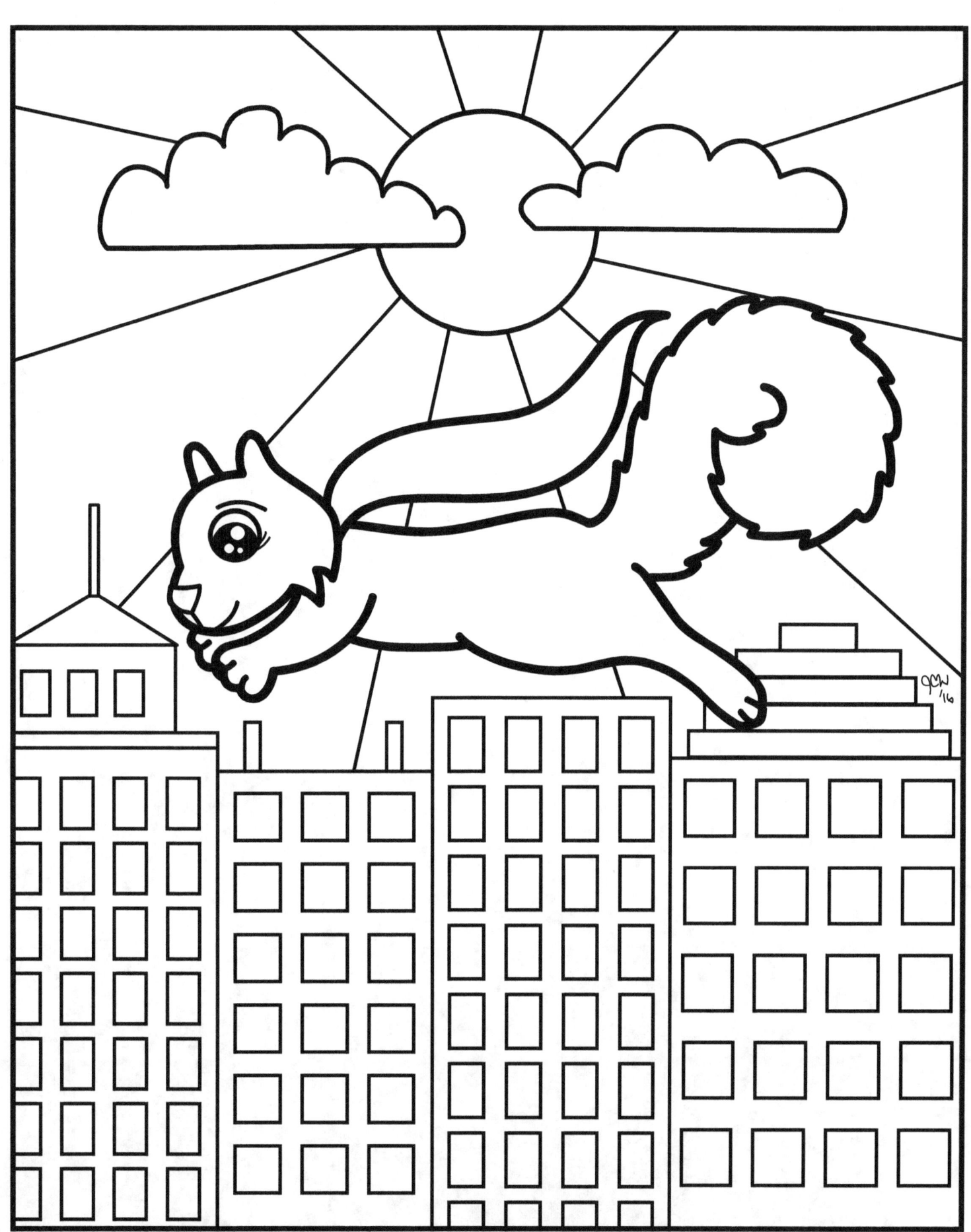

Super Squirrel

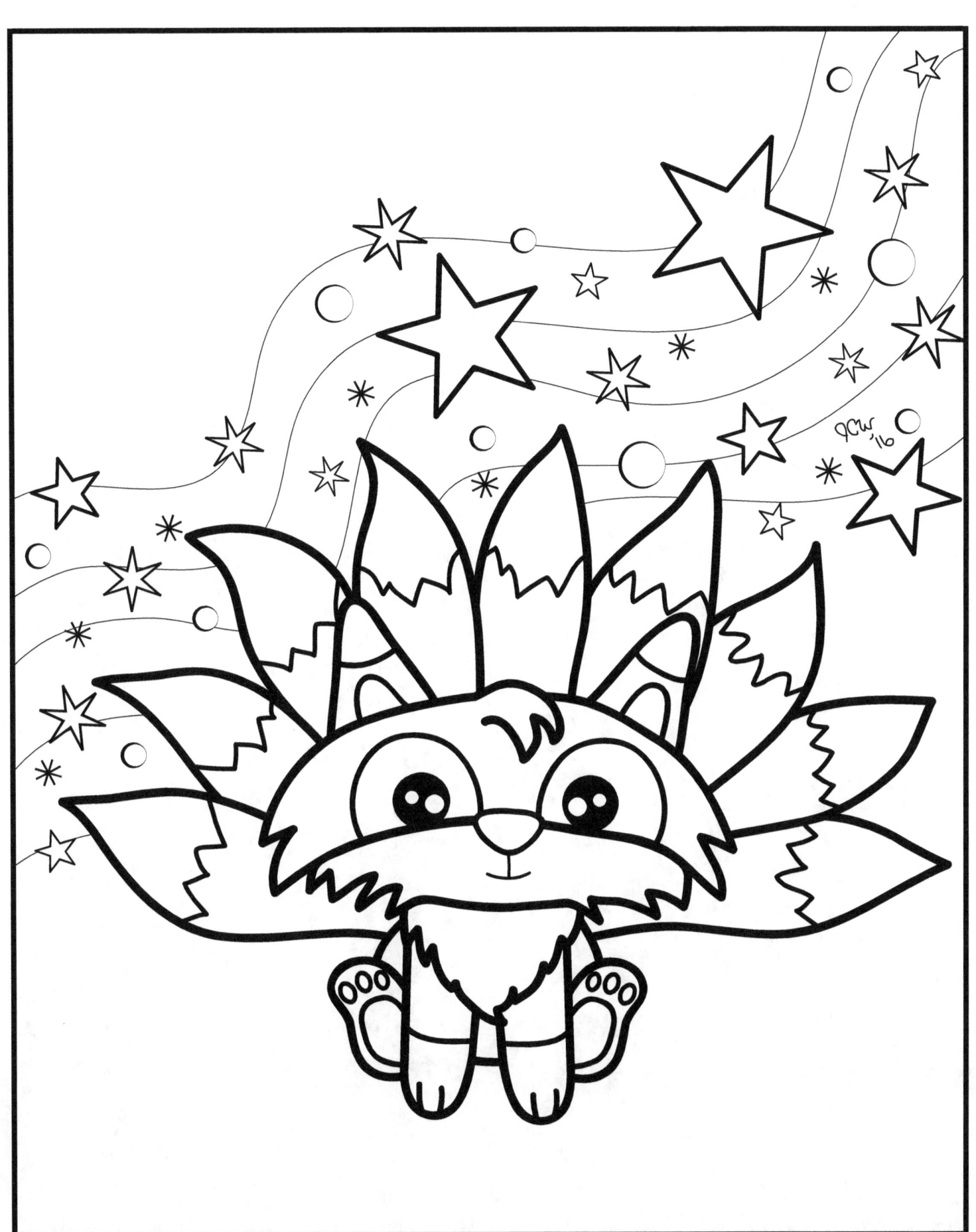

Nine-Tail Fox

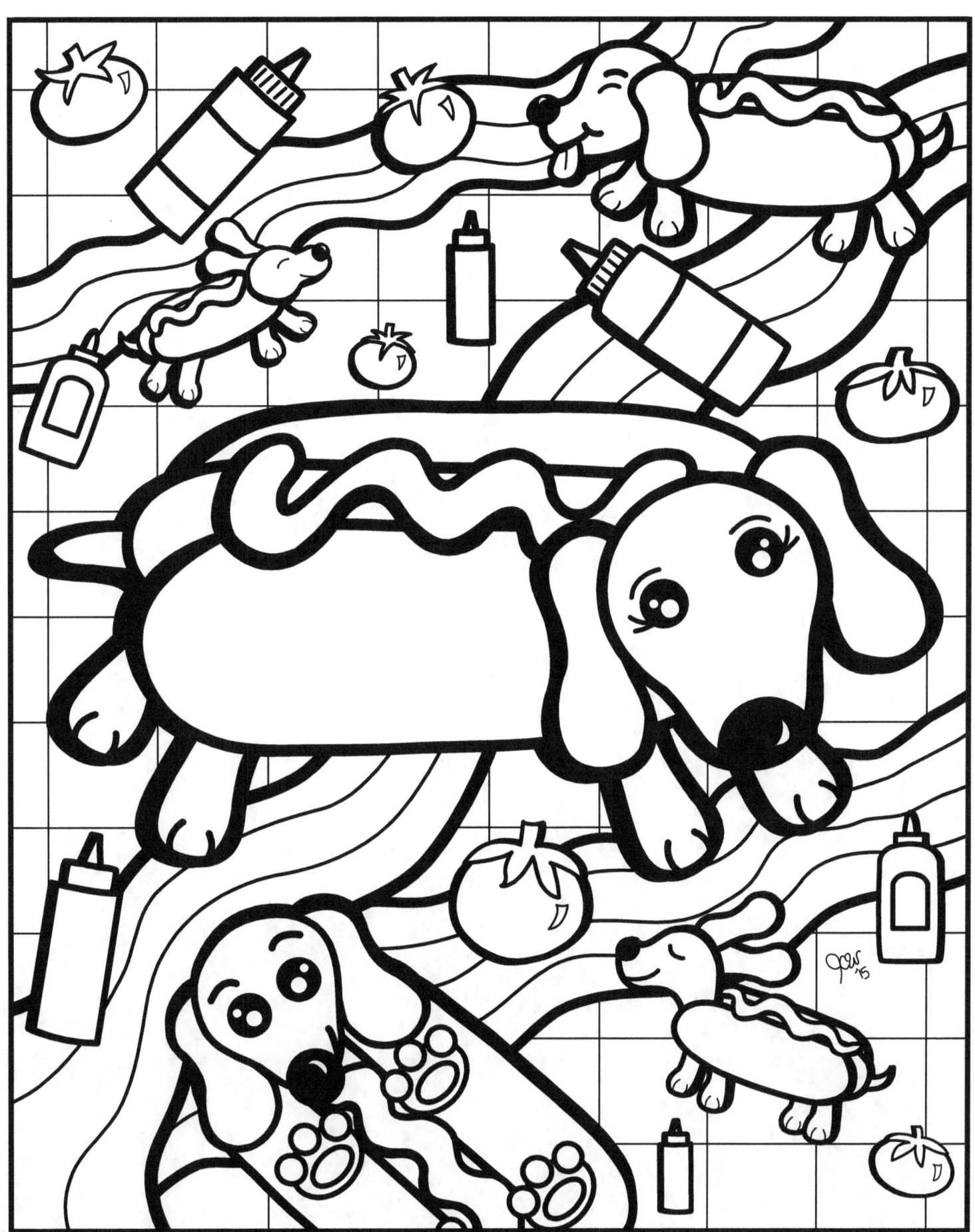

Hot Dog Dogs

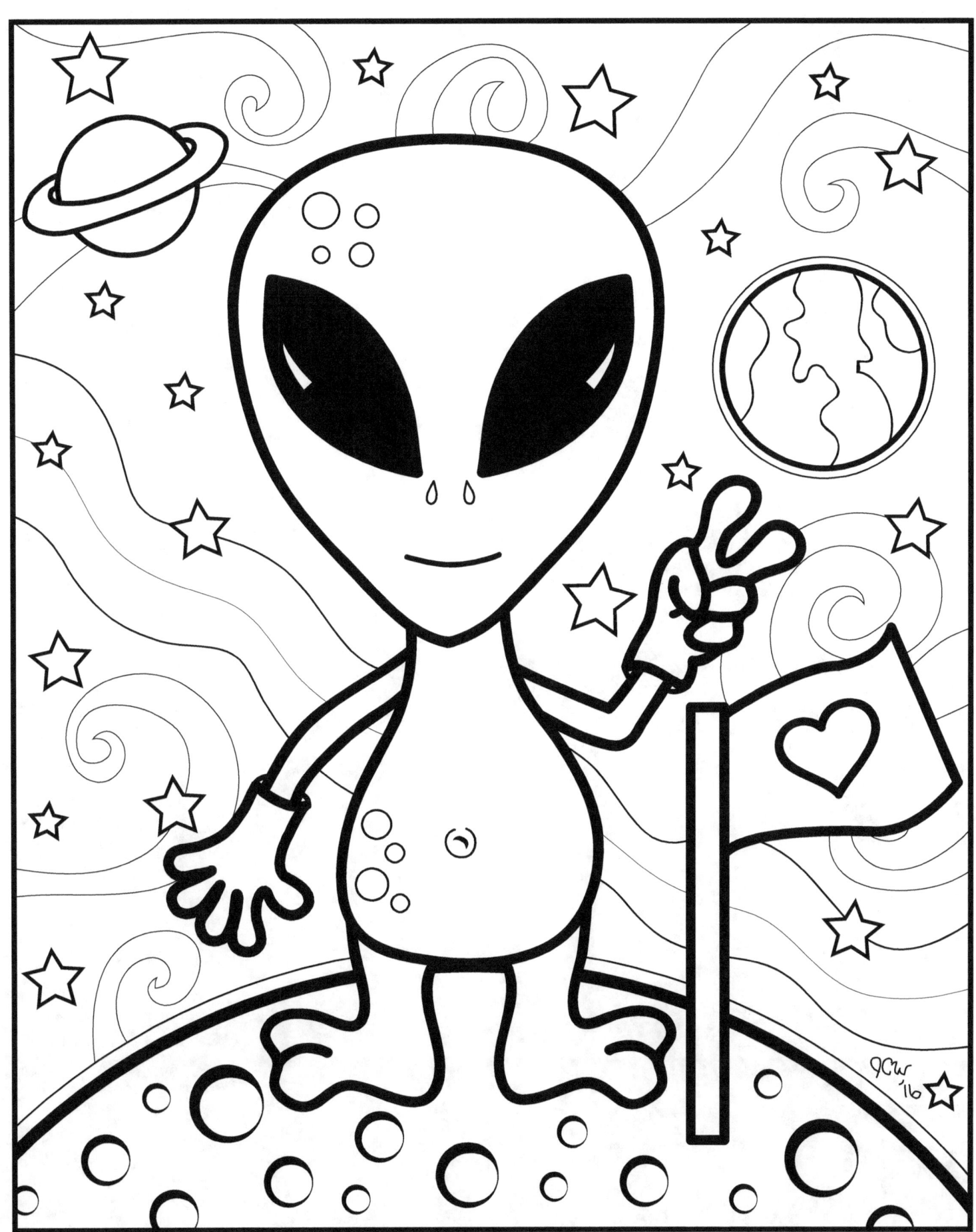

Space Alien

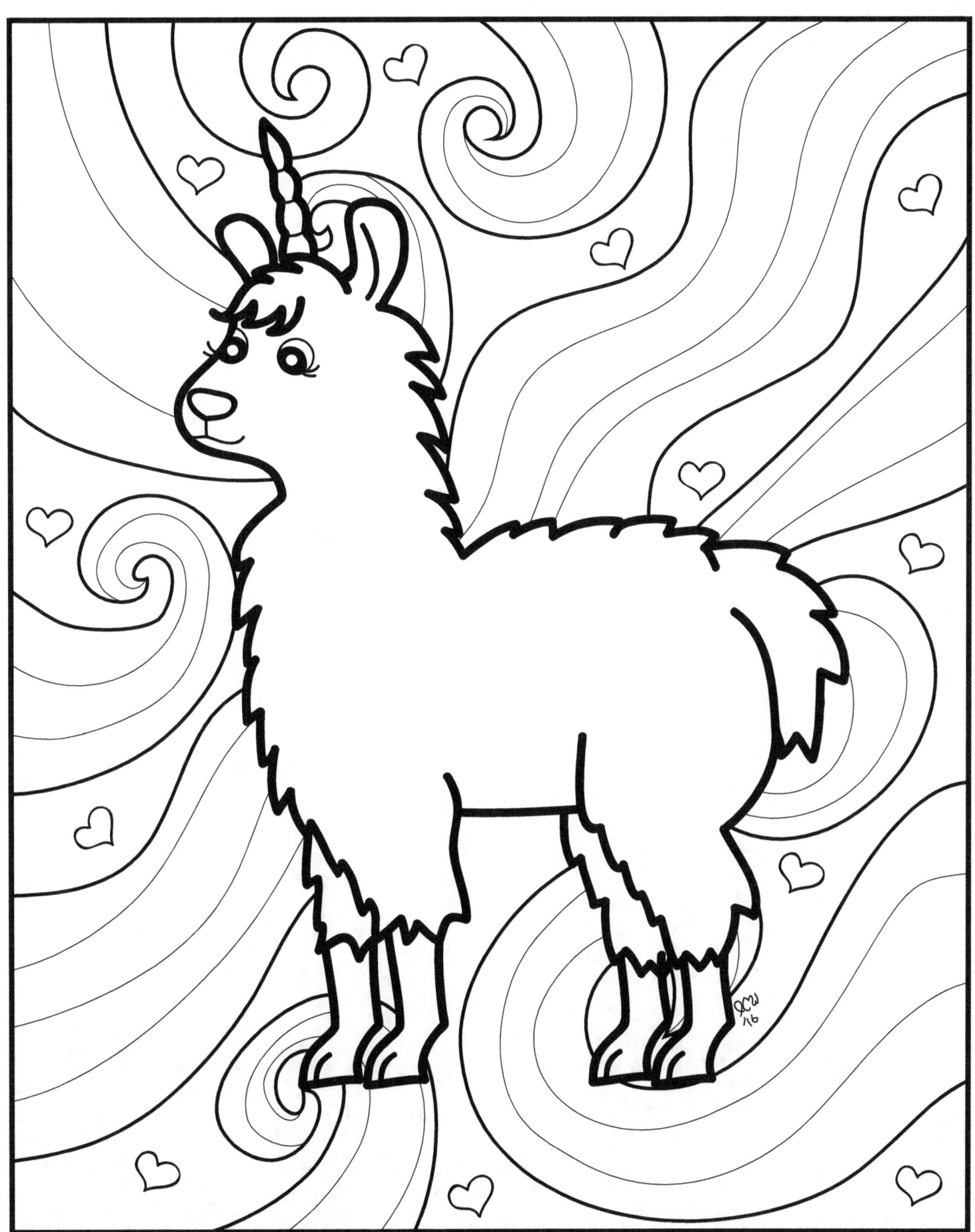

Llamacorn

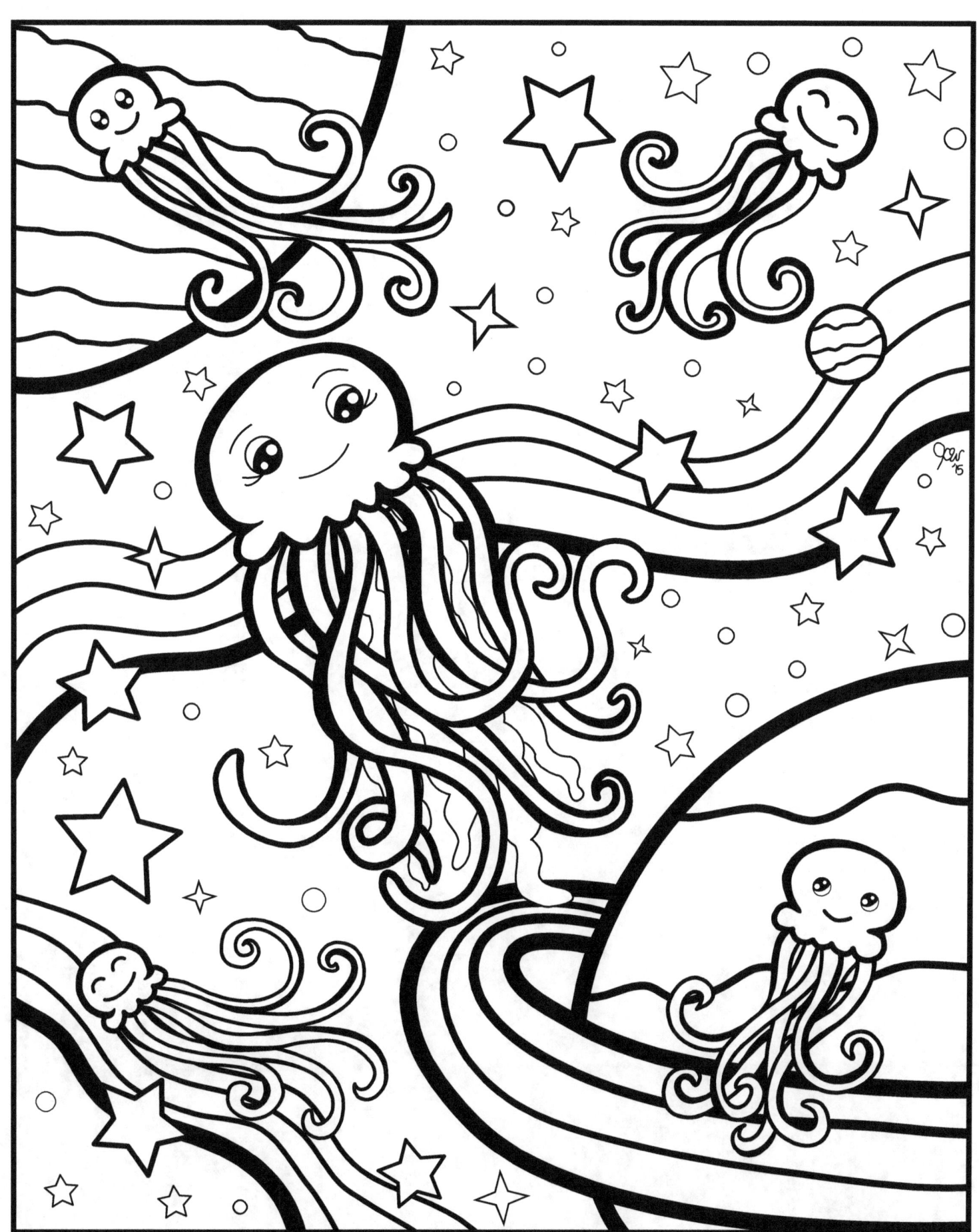

Jelly Fish in Space

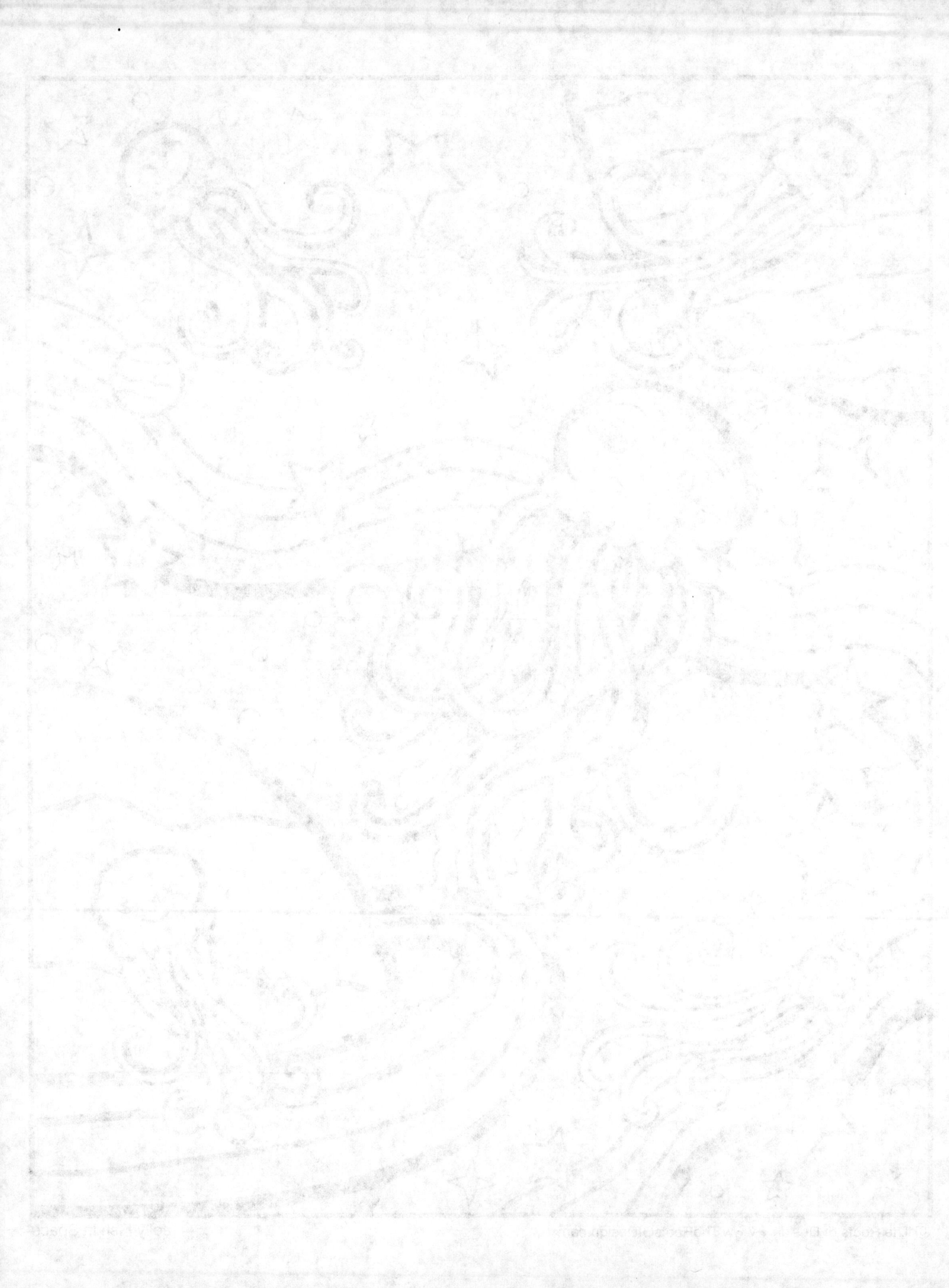

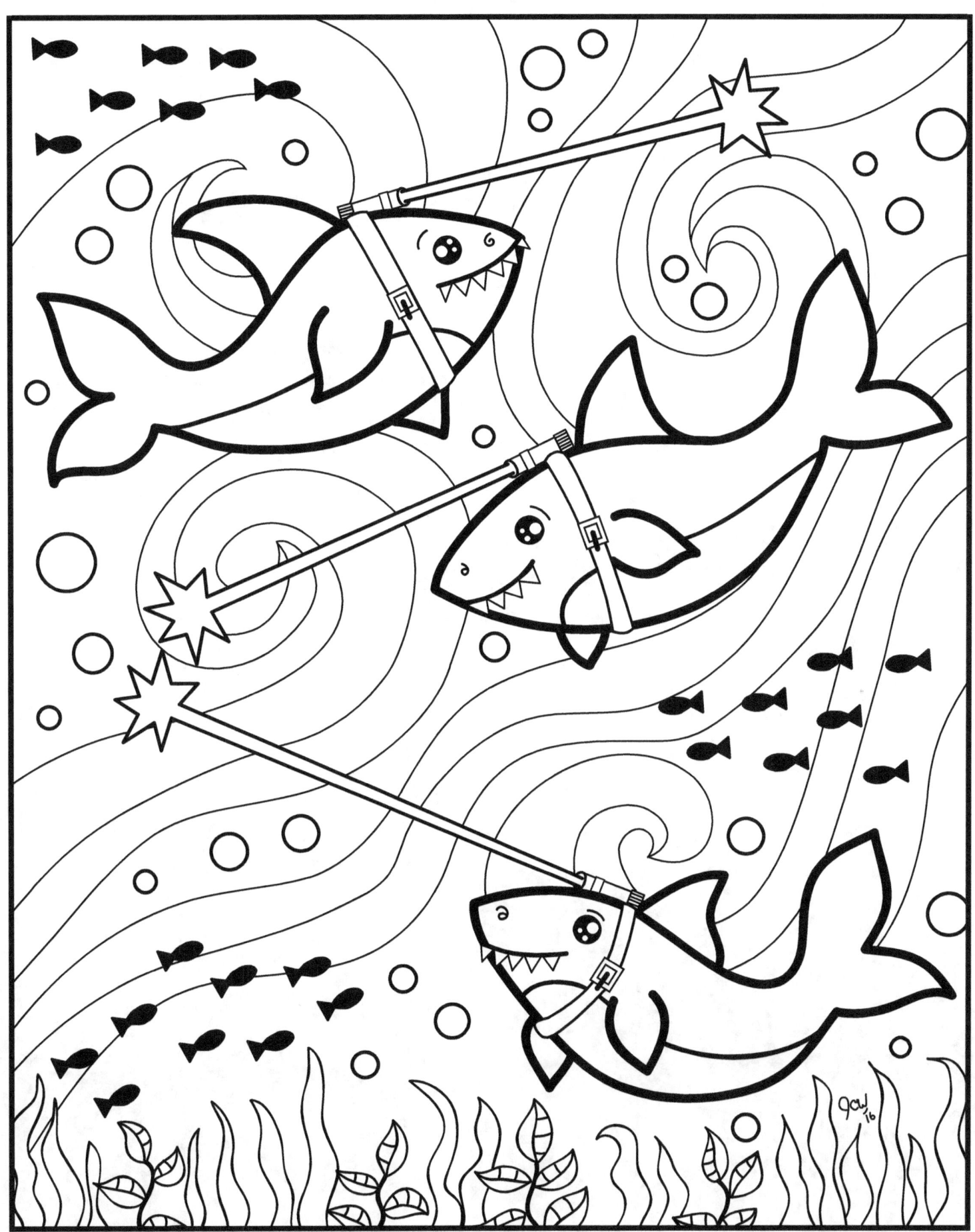

Sharks With Laser Beams

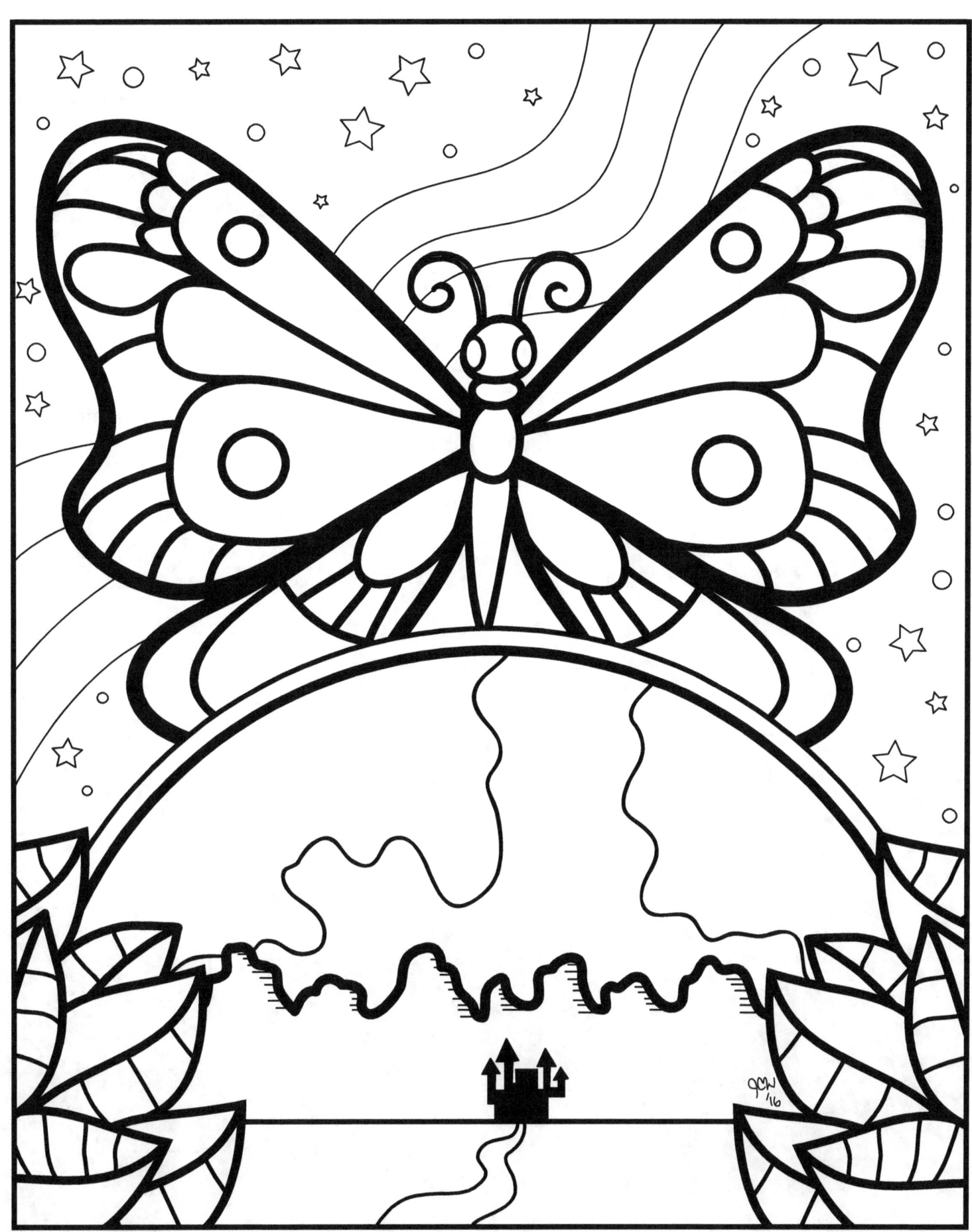

Space Butterfly

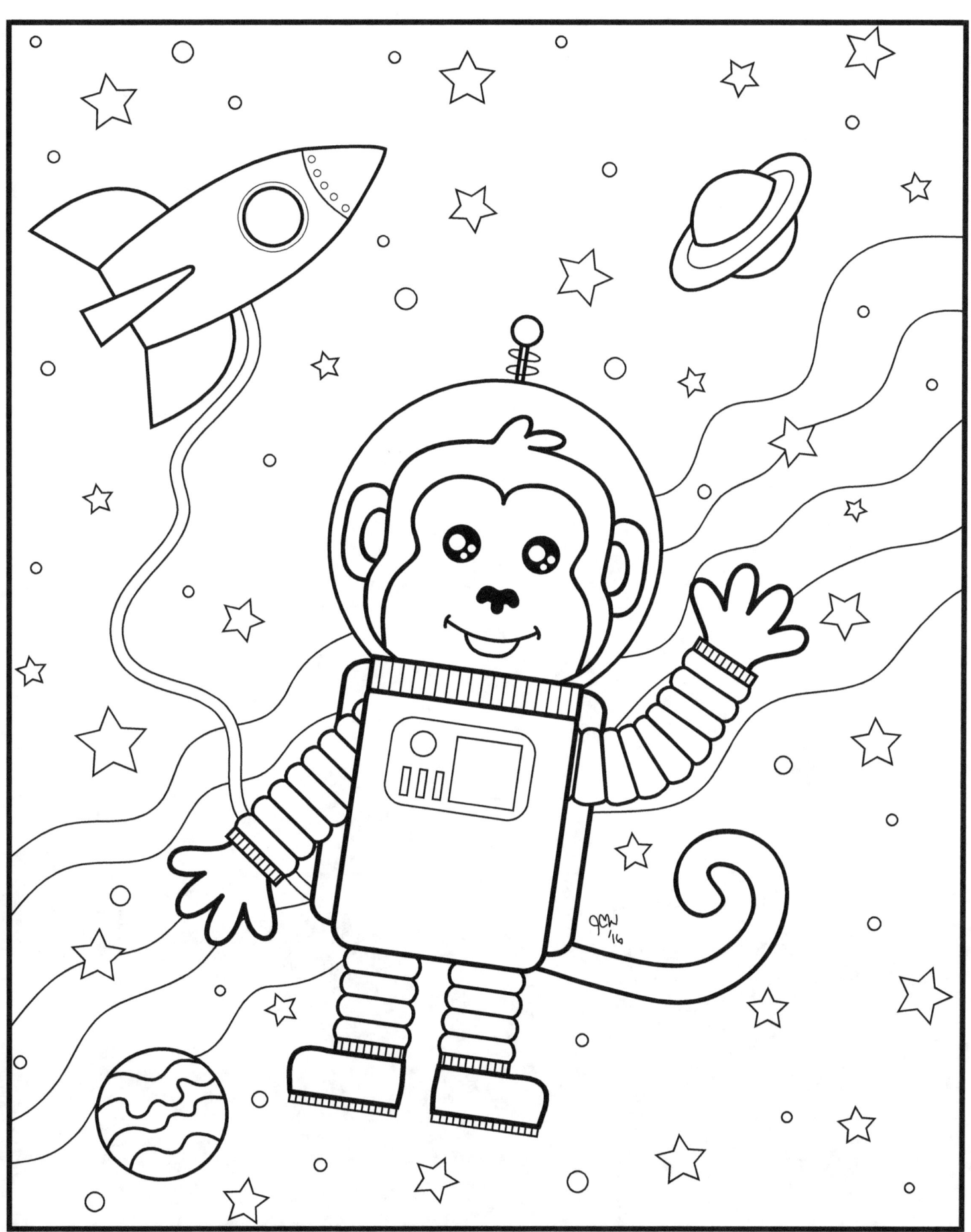

Space Monkey

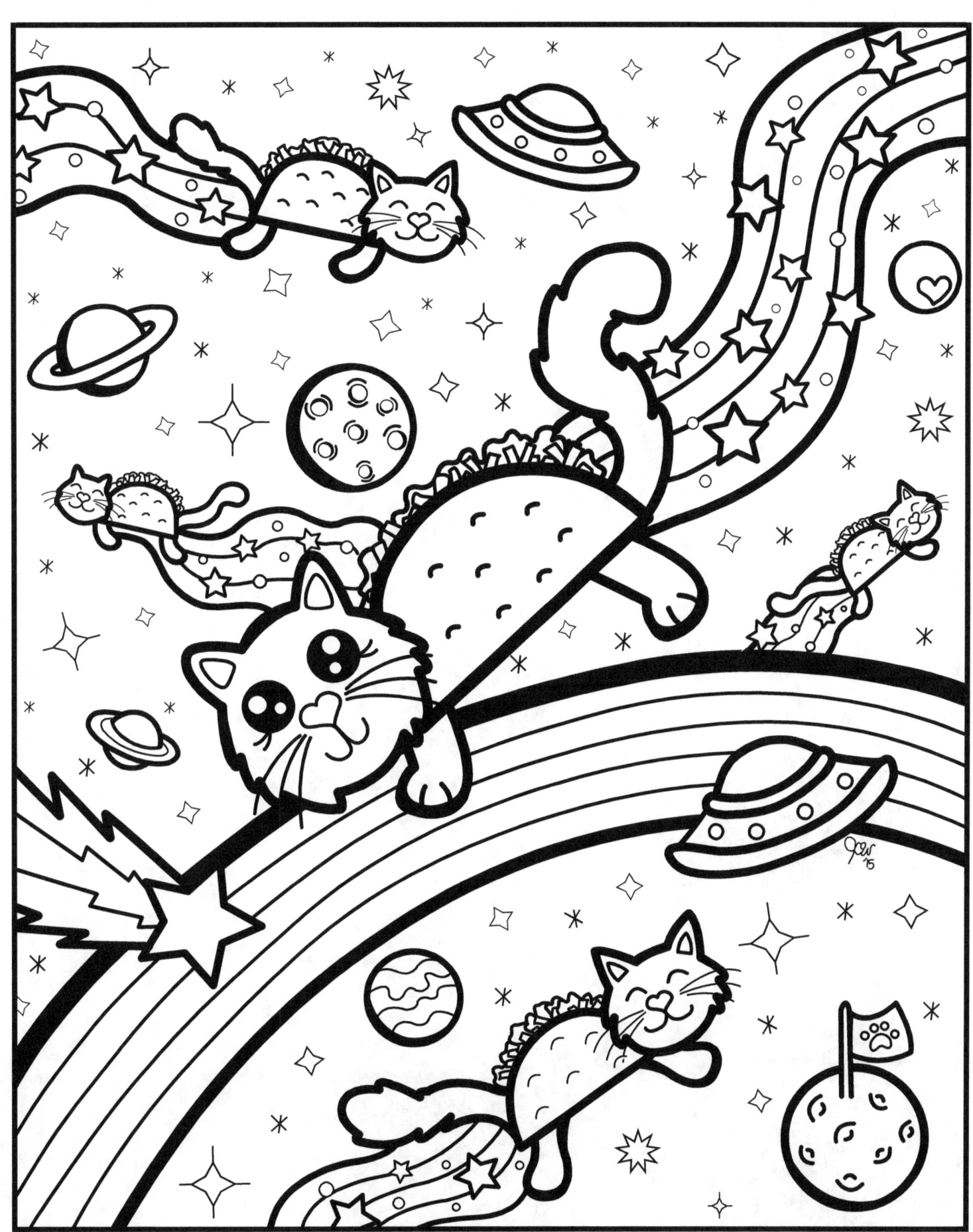

Taco Cats

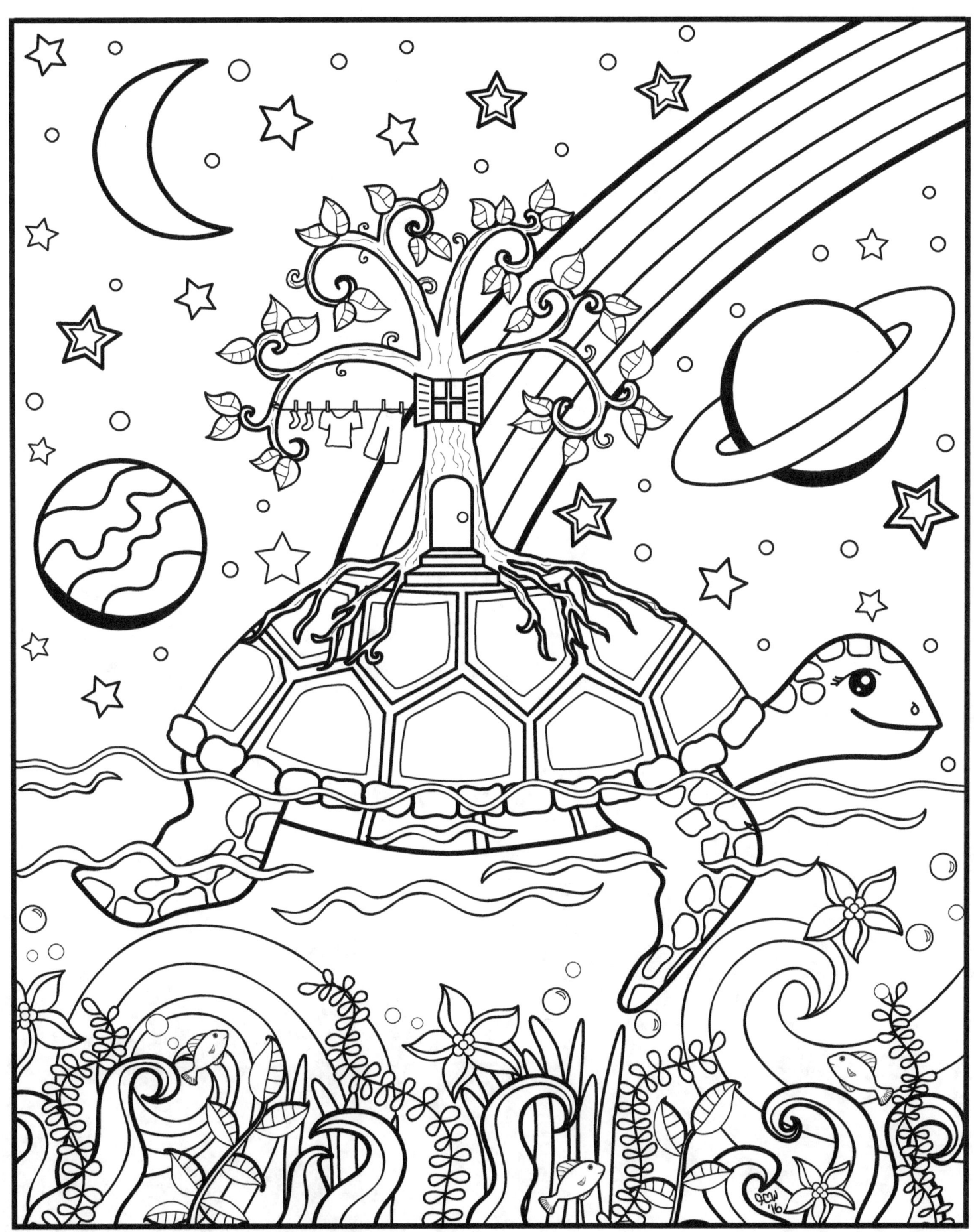

Turtle Island

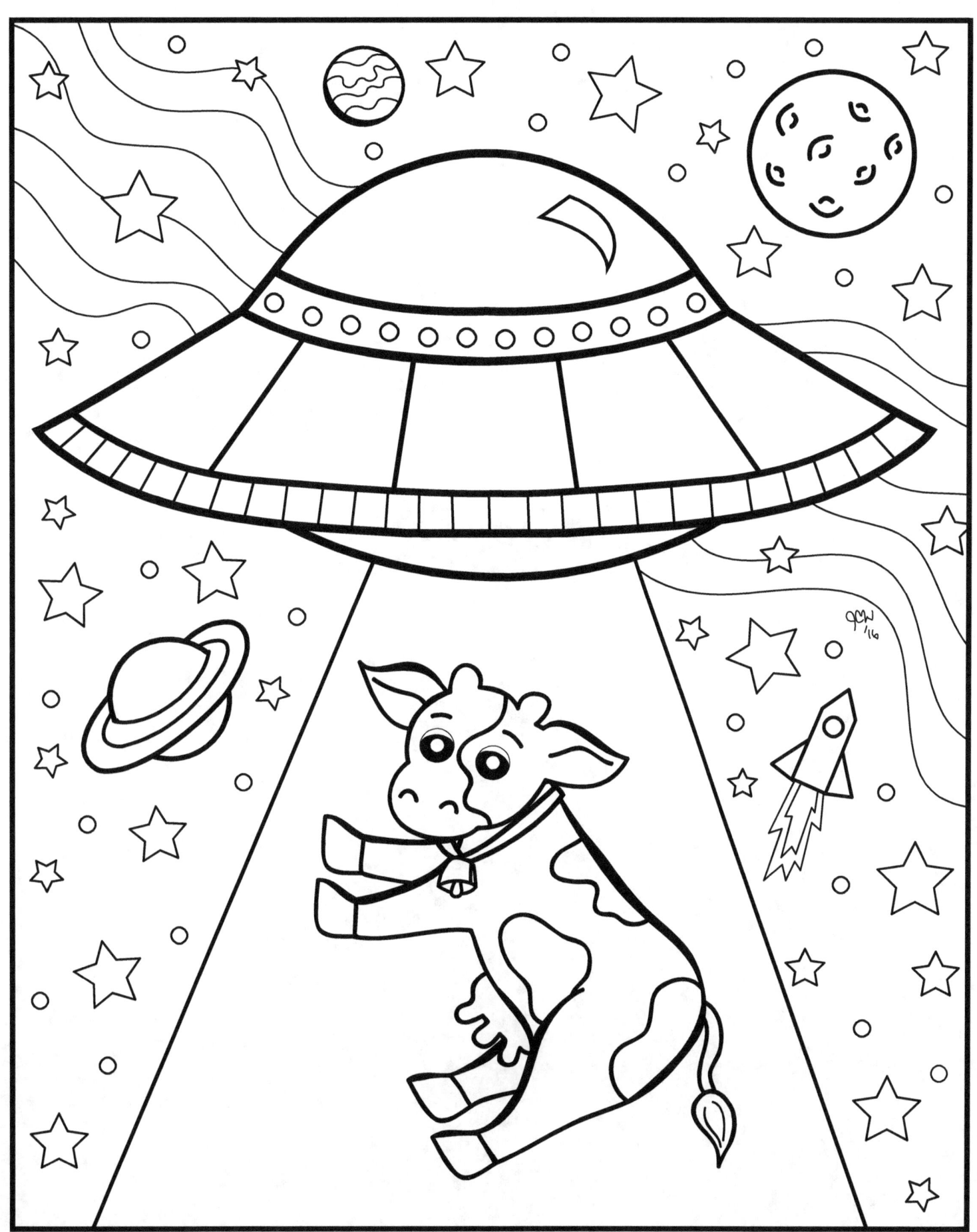

U.F.O Cow Abduction

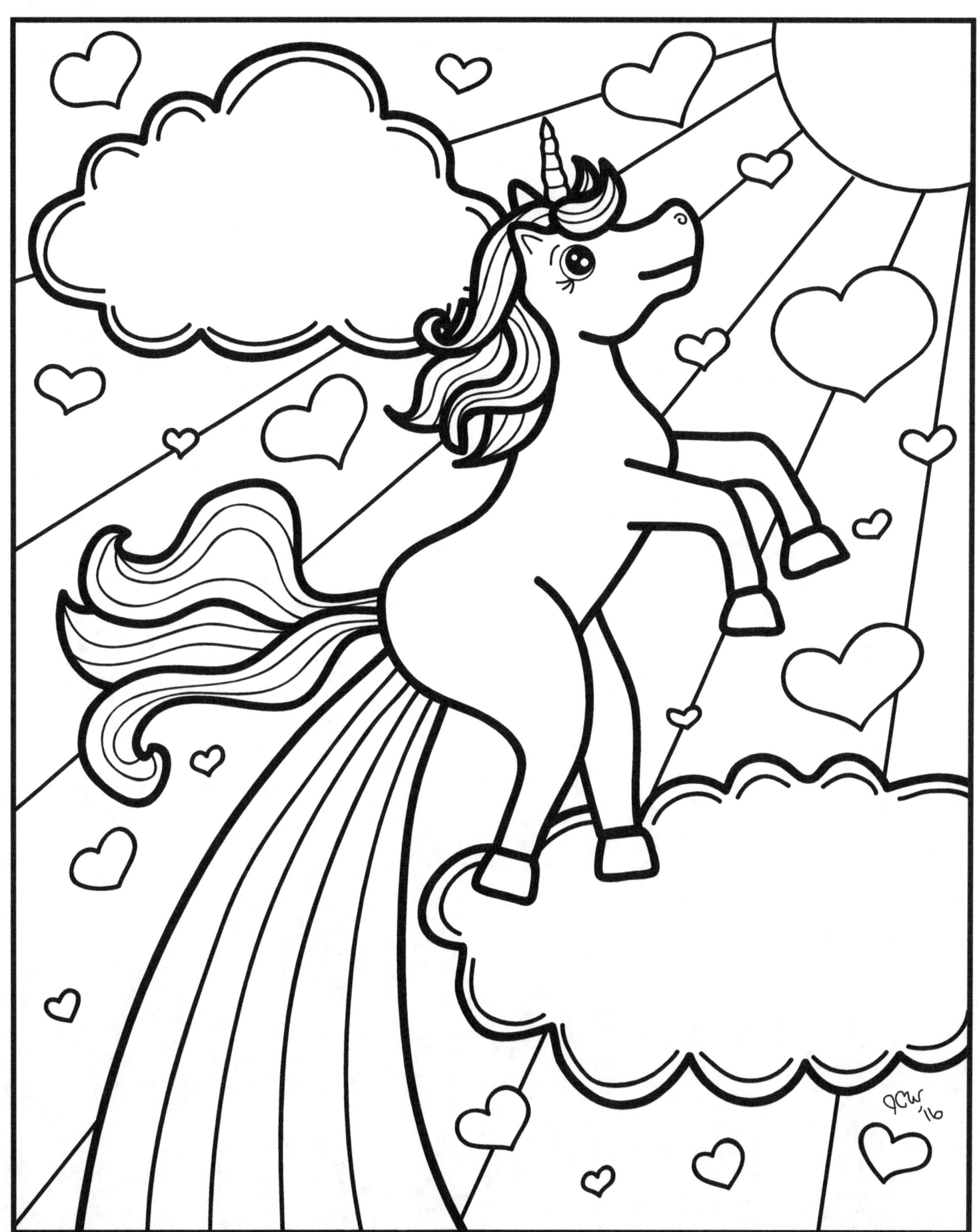

Farting Unicorn

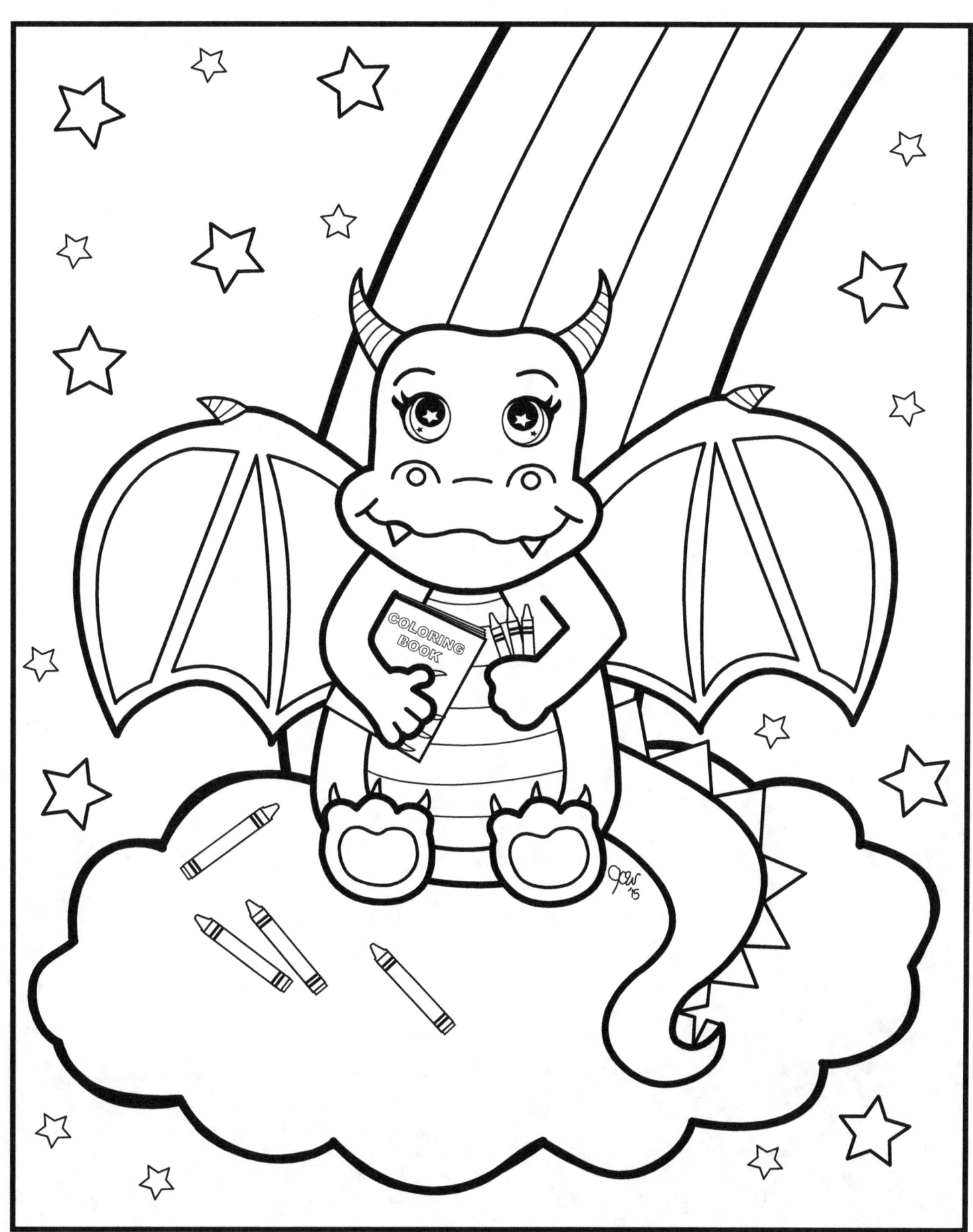

Coloring Dragon

COLORING BOOK

www.ingramcontent.com/pod-product-compliance
Lightning Source LLC
Chambersburg PA
CBHW080850170526
45158CB00009B/2698

* 9 7 8 0 9 9 6 8 4 7 9 8 8 *